Rug Hooking and
Wool Appliqué

Christine Jansen

Rug Hooking and Wool Appliqué

Christine Jansen

Schiffer Publishing Ltd

4880 Lower Valley Road · Atglen, Pennsylvania 19310

Other Schiffer Books By Christine Jansen:
How to Hook Rugs, 978-0-7643-2890-9, $14.95

Other Schiffer Books on Related Subjects:
Sewing Penny Rugs Wool Appliqué,
978-0-7643-3467-2, $12.99

The Hooker's Art: Evolving Designs in Hooked Rugs,
0-88740-459-6, $49.95

Published by Schiffer Publishing Ltd.
4880 Lower Valley Road
Atglen, PA 19310
Phone: (610) 593-1777; Fax: (610) 593-2002
E-mail: Info@schifferbooks.com

For the largest selection of fine reference books on this and related
subjects, please visit our web site at:
www.schifferbooks.com
We are always looking for people to write books on new and related
subjects. If you have an idea for a book please contact us at the above
address.

This book may be purchased from the publisher.
Include $5.00 for shipping.
Please try your bookstore first.
You may write for a free catalog.

In Europe, Schiffer books are distributed by
Bushwood Books
6 Marksbury Ave.
Kew Gardens
Surrey TW9 4JF England
Phone: 44 (0) 20 8392 8585; Fax: 44 (0) 20 8392 9876
E-mail: info@bushwoodbooks.co.uk
Website: www.bushwoodbooks.co.uk

Designed by RoS
Type set in Tekton Pro/New Baskerville BT
ISBN: 978-0-7643-3473-3
Printed in China

Acknowledgments

Since I wrote my last book a lot has happened. For one my name has changed. The last two years have had a lot of ups and downs. I went through a divorce, moved from an area where my kids and I had spent the past twenty years, and my father had a debilitating stroke. But we moved to an area we really like outside of Boston and have had a chance to travel, go to museums and really great restaurants, ski, and get together with friends and family we hadn't seen in a long while.

I want to thank my kids, Peter and Elaine, who have really had to deal with a lot this year; my mom, Tina, who took us in (including my two dogs!) and helped us to get back on our feet, for always supporting and encouraging me in all my endeavors.

I really enjoyed working on this second book. It gave me a chance to concentrate on things that I really love and hold dear. Plus, I got to meet lots of new crafters because of it.

And I couldn't do it all without the faithful and enthusiastic love of my two dogs. Dooney and Loden get me out in the morning for our three-mile walk and love to curl up with me when I'm working on a rug. There is nothing like doggy kisses to keep you going.

Dooney

Loden

Contents

Introduction: Busy Hands Are Happy Hands

My first "rug" ...

I have always loved making things. My Aunt Phyllis was a great inspiration to me. Next to my grandmother, she was the best cook I have ever met. Besides cooking, my Aunt Phyllis could sew, knit, do crewelwork, garden, paint ... In short, my Aunt Phyllis could do everything! One day she was working on a latch hook wall hanging. I was so enthused that she bought me a kit and we finished my first "rug." My mother has had it in her downstairs bathroom for the past forty years!

I earned my degree in culinary arts, but continued with sewing and painting. When I became a stay at home mom, I taught decorative painting and faux finishes at a local community school.

I never kept up with latch hooking, but many years ago a student showed me a project she was working on. It was a Claire Murray rug of a Cape Cod cottage. My heart started beating faster and fireworks exploded in my head! This was incredible! Oh my goodness — the softness of the yarn, the gorgeous design, the simple technique! How had I not discovered rug hooking before! It was so beautiful and so easy. I immediately went to a Claire Murray store and bought a kit. I was in heaven! That rug is still a favorite sleeping spot for my dogs.

Chapter One: Hooking and Dyeing Materials

An assortment of yarns and wools.

Wool

Yarn

Wool yarn is my favorite hooking material. It's what I first started with and still love. It's easy to dye although it readily comes in many colors, it's a nice long length so there's not a lot of stopping and starting and it's ready to go once you wind the skein into a ball. When choosing wool yarns, choose bulky or worsted weight. For projects that are not going to be walked on, the new specialty yarns can add some pizzazz to areas of your project.

Wools of different textures.

Fabric

Wool fabric is the most commonly used fabric. New wool off the bolt is wonderful but a less expensive source of wool is old clothes. A great source for old clothes is thrift shops and yard sales. When looking for wool clothing, look for 100% wool, medium weight; not light weight or winter coat weight. Do not use gabardine, which unravels easily. When you get home, immediately put the clothes in your washer with hot water and a little liquid detergent. Unfortunately you don't know what kind of insects might have gotten into the clothes. If you can't wash it right away, put the clothing into a garbage bag with mothballs until you are able to wash it.

It doesn't matter where you have gotten your wool; the preparation is the same. All wool needs to shrink to keep it from unraveling. Wash the wool in your washing machine on a hot setting with a little detergent. Wash same colors together and rinse with cold water. When the cycle is finished toss the wool in the dryer and dry until it is slightly damp. Do not over dry.

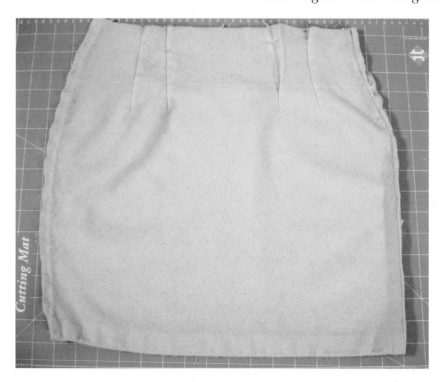

Deconstruct wool clothing found at yard sales or thrift shops.

Dyeing Your Wool

The great thing about dyeing your own wool is that the more mottled the color comes out, the better so you don't have to become a professional at dyeing. The mottled color gives the rug so much character and personality giving you a lot of leeway. Plus if you get a color you don't like, you can over-dye it and change its personality completely.

There are several places to get dye for rug hooking. See Resources at the end of this book. Read the instructions for the dye that you purchase. The following are general directions.

Equipment for Dyeing

There are many books available on dyeing wool. Check with your local library or online for books and recipes for dyes. *NOTE: The equipment you use for dyeing should NEVER be used for food!*

- A large enamel or stainless steel pot
- Glass measuring cup or small enamel pot
- Dye
- White vinegar
- Measuring spoons
- Long handled tongs (for stirring/flipping)
- Apron
- Rubber gloves

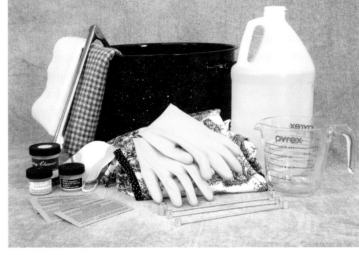

Dyeing equipment featured are various dyes, wool, large pot, mask, gloves, apron, measuring spoons, vinegar, and measuring cup.

Dyeing Yarn

1. Coil into a large loose circle, tie each quadrant with a scrap of yarn.
2. Presoak your material by adding a little dish detergent to warm water and soak for 30 minutes. I use a gallon storage bag if I'm doing small amounts.
3. Donning your apron and gloves, follow the directions on your dye package to dissolve dye.
4. Fill your large pot with approximately enough water to cover your wool. Add your dye and bring the water to a boil.
5. Slowly add your wool. Stir constantly for a more even color. Don't stir for a more mottled look.
6. Add the vinegar according to the dye packet. When the water has cleared, all the dye has been absorbed.
7. "Cook" the wool for 1/2 hour. Remove the pot from the heat.
8. Rinse the wool first in hot water, then bringing it slowly to cool water. Alternately, you could let it cool in the pot overnight. Rinse the wool in your washing machine on the rinse setting.

   YARN ONLY: After removing from the washer, take your yarn into the backyard. Holding one of the tied ends, swing the yarn firmly in a circle to remove excess water. The yarn should make a "whizzing" sound as you swing it.

9. Dry in your dryer on medium heat. Add a towel or two to the dryer so that the wool moves around. Yarn should be put in a lingerie bag to prevent excessive tangling. Check the dryer every 15 minutes to make sure the yarn doesn't over-dry.

Chapter Two: Rug Hooking

Rug hooking takes a few basic supplies: backing fabric, hooking tool, and wool. There are projects in this book to get you started. After that, you are only limited by your own imagination.

Backing Fabrics

The backing fabric is the material that your design will go on. Your backing fabric needs to be at least 8" larger in width and in depth than your pattern to leave a 4" margin on each side. It also needs to have an open weave that will allow the hook to pass through the hole.

Listed below are descriptions of the common materials used for backing fabric. Try each one and decide which is best for you.

Burlap

Many years ago grain was bought in large burlap sacks. Thrifty New Englanders used these sacks as the backing for their rugs. Over time it was found that burlap sacking doesn't last and begins to break down over time. Today there are much better fabrics to use as backing.

Scottish burlap is an oil treated, evenly woven mesh. It tends to be a little rough when hooking and sheds small fibers, which can become a little annoying. This is the least expensive of the backings. Do not purchase Angus burlap, which is more commonly found in stores. This burlap does not have an even weave, is very rough, and is used for wrapping the root balls of trees.

Scottish burlap is versatile and will hold finer strips, but is also great for primitive hooking with large strips.

Monk's Cloth

Monk's cloth is a soft, heavy, and 100% cotton. It usually has a white grid every 2" that will help keep your lines straighter. Very important is the size of the holes: buy cloth that has 12 holes per inch (12 count). Any less and your strips will not stay in.

Monk's cloth comes in sizes up to 72" and 144" and is a moderately priced backing. It works well with either narrow or wide strips.

Linen

Linen is very strong and easy to work on. It is usually the most expensive. A very pliant foundation, it will last forever. The mesh opening is suitable for wool strips from 5/32" to 3/8" wide.

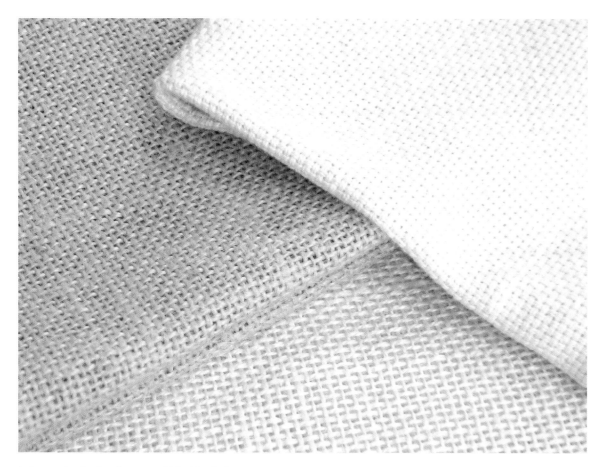

Left to right: Burlap, Linen, and Monk's cloth.

Close up of Monk's cloth.

Tools and Supplies

Handles

Rug hooking tools come in different sizes with different handles. Basically a rug hook is a crochet hook with a wooden handle. The hook ranges from fine (for thinner strips) to very coarse or primitive (for thicker strips). Start out with a medium size hook. As you progress you can try the finer size or the more primitive size hooks depending on what type of hooking you prefer.

The handles vary from bulb shape to pencil shape to a variety of ergonomically correct shapes. You'll find handles made from some very exotic wood, for a price, of course! It's a good idea to have more than one shape handle. During long hooking sessions switch between the two intermittently to prevent hand cramps.

Shank size is important too. The shank is the area between the handle and the hook. If you are working with a larger cut strip, a large shank will open up the hole for you to pull the loop through.

Frames and Hoops

The frame or hoop will keep the backing taut while you hook. This is necessary for nice, even loops. If you're not sure about rug hooking as a hobby, start out with a large quilting hoop.

Rug hooking frames are usually rectangular with gripper strips on all sides. They come in all sizes. I have a sit-on rug frame that I love. It swivels easily and lets me get comfortable when I hook. If you're in the market for a rug-hooking frame, search the Internet for all different varieties.

Gripper frame and quilting hoop.

14

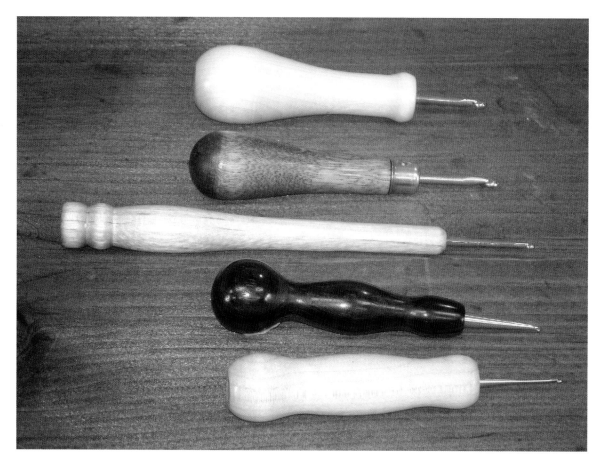

Here are various hook sizes with different types of handles.

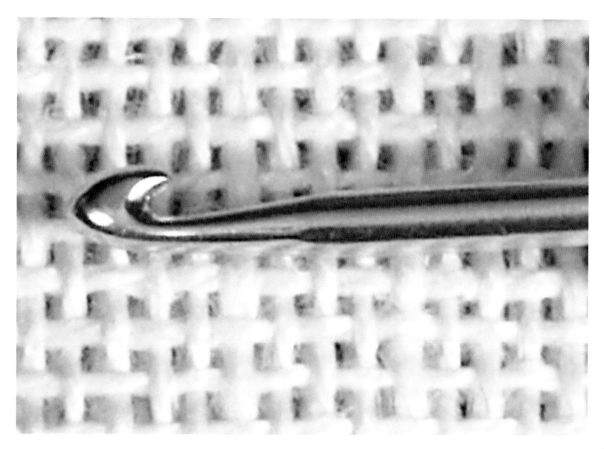

Close up of hook end.

Other Supplies

Red Dot Tracer

This is a non-woven tracing material with red dots marking each square inch. The red dots help you keep your patterns straight. This material is thin enough for a marker to go through onto your backing fabric. You'll find it at most fabric stores.

Permanent Marker

You will need a permanent maker such as Sharpie® Fine Point. Have two different colors of markers. If you make a mistake as you are drawing your pattern onto your backing make the correction in a different color marker.

Circle Beam Compass

I found this nifty tool at Staples and I love it. It lets me make any size circle up to 24".

Scissors

A sharp pair of scissors are necessary for cutting your tails without pulling loops out. Embroidery scissors will help you lift any lower loops to the height of the other loops. Appliqué scissors lay flat on your rug to cut off tails.

Cording

If you choose to use cording to finish your rugs you can purchase cotton clothesline between 1/4" and 1/2".

Red dot tracer, cording, compass, appliqué scissors, black marker, and embroidery scissors.

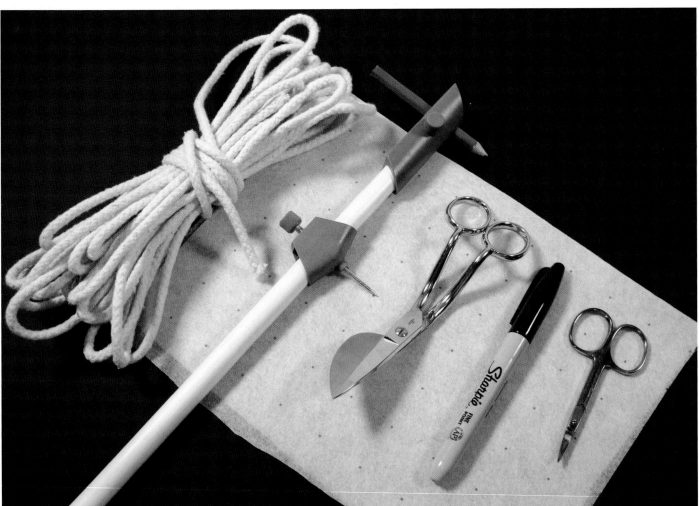

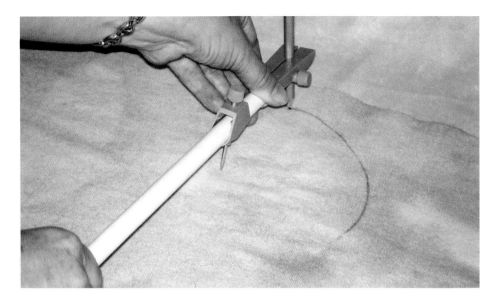

This easy-to-use compass is for drawing the perfect circles.

Embroidery scissors lifting a loop.

Appliqué scissors lay flat for cutting tails.

Cutting the Wool

In general, you need approximately four times as much wool as the area that you are hooking. When you have been hooking for a while, you will be able to determine if you need more or less.

If you are doing a sky or any type of large background, use several slightly different shades of a color. Cut several strips of each and mix them up; then blindly pull from your pile. This adds character to your piece, giving it a nice mottled background.

In order to hook the wool, we will need strips — *many, many strips*. Don't get ahead of yourself, though; you want to cut as you go. Wool is valuable and, if you have already cut a pile of 4/32" and then decide an area would look better in a 6/32", you may not have enough wool to be able to cut more for your project.

Strips are cut into 32nds of an inch up to 8. If the instructions call for a #6 cut, the strips will be 6/32". A #8 cut is 8/32" or ¼". There are several ways to cut the wool, but you will first need to square up your wool. Snip into your wool about 2" from the selvage edge (the edge that is woven so it won't unravel). Take each side of the tear in your hands and rip. The wool will tear on the straight of the grain. Your strips MUST to be on the straight of the grain or they will be weak — and weak strips can tear when you hook them or when the finished rug is walked on.

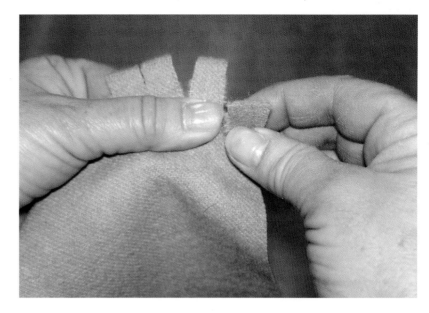

The least expensive method is to tear all of your strips. This is great for primitive rugs that use a #8 (1/4"), #9 (3/8") or #10 (1/2"). Just snip your fabric in the desired increments and tear away. *Note: #8.5, #9, and #10 do not follow the 32ⁿᵈ of an inch rule.* Here, I'm cutting the wool in 1/2" increments and tearing.

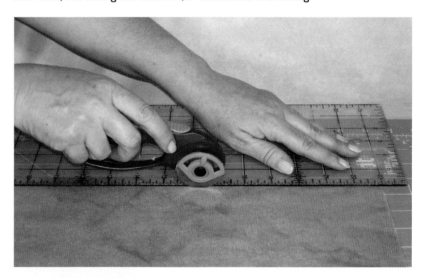

Another inexpensive way to cut wool is with a rotary cutter, a cutting mat, and a see-thru acrylic ruler. Place your wool on the cutting mat and place your ruler on the appropriate fraction of an inch lined up with the torn edge of the wool. Cut several strips and flip your wool so you begin cutting from the other torn edge.

A little more costly, but much easier way to cut wool is with a wool cutter. There are several good brands available. I use the Fraser Model 500-1 (shown here). It's easy to change the cutting heads to different widths for different size strips. *Note: When changing colors on your cutter, a blast of canned air (found in stationary stores) will remove the wool residue.*

Transferring the Pattern

First you will need the pattern to be the correct size. On a copy machine, enlarge the pattern to fit your need. To enlarge something as large as a rug you will have to enlarge the pattern in sections and then piece the pattern together. If your copier will not enlarge large enough you may have to take the pattern to a copy shop.

Enlarging Your Pattern

1. Measure your piece diagonally from corner to corner and then …
2. Measure your pattern diagonally from corner to corner.
3. Divide the number of inches you want the pattern to be by the number of inches the pattern is.
4. The "quotient" is the number you set the copier to enlarge the pattern: i.e. desired size is 21" if pattern is 17" — 21 ÷ 17 = 1.23, set the copier to 123%.

Decreasing Your Pattern

1. Measure your piece diagonally from corner to corner and then …
2. Measure your pattern diagonally from corner to corner.
3. Divide the number of inches the pattern is by the number of inches you want.
4. The "quotient" is the number you set the copier on to decrease the pattern: i.e. desired size is 17", but pattern is 21" — 17 ÷ 21 = .82, set the copier to 82%.

Tracing Your Pattern

Red Dot Tracer

Once you have the pattern to the correct size, tape it to a flat surface such as a table or a hard floor. Place the Red Dot Tracer on top of the pattern and tape or pin the Tracer securely. Make sure the red dots line up on any straight lines in the pattern. With the marker, trace all of the pattern onto the Red Dot Tracer.

Now tape your backing fabric to the table. Lay the Red Dot Tracer pattern on the backing fabric leaving approximately 4" on each side for the hoop or frame. Make sure the straight lines of your pattern follow the straight lines of your fabric grain. Tape or pin securely. I use a lot of long hatpins.

Trace over the pattern slowly, so that the marker flows through the tracer and onto your backing fabric. Lift a corner of the tracer and make sure your lines are visible. Go over any that are not visible. Use a ruler for straight lines. If your pattern is too light when you remove the Red Dot, just go over the lines with your marker.

Trace your pattern onto the Red Dot Tracer.

Place the Red Dot Tracer onto your backing fabric and go over your lines slowly with the marker.

Lift to make sure the marker is going through.

Light Box Tracer

Another way to trace your pattern onto the backing is with a light box tracer. These are small rectangular acrylic boxes with a light bulb inside. This method is good for smaller projects such as the ornaments. Light boxes can be found at craft or art supply stores and are relatively inexpensive. I find I use mine a lot.

Tape your pattern to the light box; then place your backing fabric over the pattern and secure. Trace with the black marker.

Finishing the Edges

Once your pattern is traced on, you will need to prevent the backing from unraveling. You can either zigzag a stitch around the edge or, if you're lucky enough to have a serger, serge the edges.

Another way to finish the edges is with 2" tape — masking, painters, or duct. Place 1" on your edge and fold the other inch to the back.

Taping, serging, and zigzag stitching prevents unraveling.

21

Hooking Your Rug

You are going to hook from the center out:

Place the center of your project in the center of your frame or hoop.

Gently pull the fabric side-to-side and top-to-bottom, so that it is taut and straight.

From there:

With the hook in your dominant hand and the strip/yarn underneath the backing fabric, stick the hook through a hole, wrap the yarn or wool strip over the hook, and pull up the yarn or wool strip through the hole about 1" above the fabric. Keep the strip/yarn in your other hand under the fabric. The first time you are just bringing up the tail.

Push your hook through a hole.

Lift up the first tail.

Secure over the grippers — the gripper will hold your fabric securely in place.

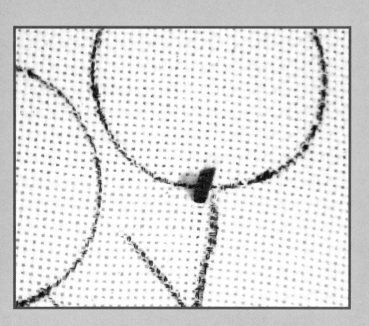

Leave about 1" of tail.

Stick the hook into the second hole and repeat to make a loop. The loop should be about 1/4" high off your fabric. The "rule" is the height of the loop is the same as the width of the strip. If it is more than this, give a little tug with your left hand to bring it down to the right height. The underside of the loop should be snug against your backing fabric.

When picking the next hole to stick your hook into, you want your loops to be touching each other, but not crushing each other. If your loops are drooping over, they are too close. Keep hooking until you need to change color. Skip to the second or third hole for the next loop. Pull that final loop up higher than the others and cut the loop leaving a tail on top and pulling the rest of the strip out from the bottom. If you run out of a strip pull the final bit on top to make a tail. Your next color (or same color if you ran out) will start in the same hole that your last one left off. Two tails will come out of one hole on top of your project.

NOTE: Unless the instructions say otherwise, hook just inside the black drawn line. Outline an area first and fill in.

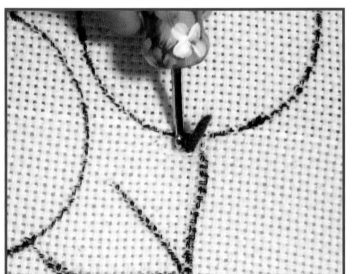

Push the hook through the next hole.

Bring up a loop to approximately 1/4".

Bringing up the next loop.

Now you're hooking a rug!

Make sure your non-hooking hand is keeping the strip straight underneath the backing. You don't want any twisted loops at the top or bottom. Twists or lumps on the bottom will loosen the individual threads of the strip as the rug is walked on and the rug will start to wear in that area.

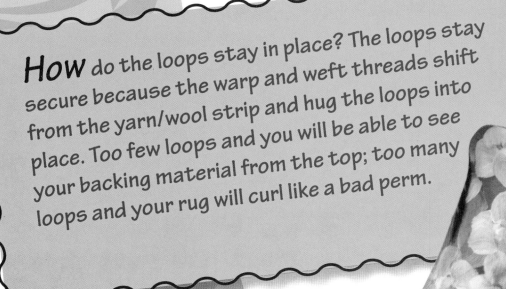

The back should be smooth and neat.

HOW do the loops stay in place? The loops stay secure because the warp and weft threads shift from the yarn/wool strip and hug the loops into place. Too few loops and you will be able to see your backing material from the top; too many loops and your rug will curl like a bad perm.

Hooking Backgrounds

"Meandering" is filling in the background with swirls and spirals.

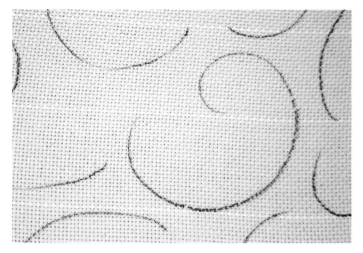

If you are a beginner, draw the swirls and spirals, randomly, on your background with the black marker.

With one color, hook right onto the spiral that you have drawn.

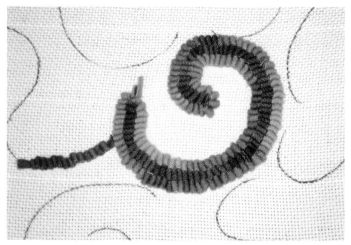

If you are using more than one shade of a color, hook a spiral first and then outline your spiral with a second color.

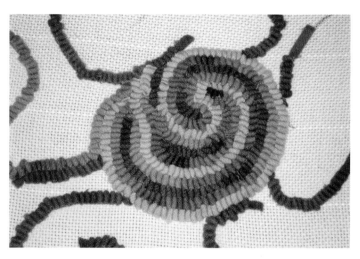

You can continue with a third color or repeat with your first color; continue until your background is filled in.

Done… You now have a meandered background.

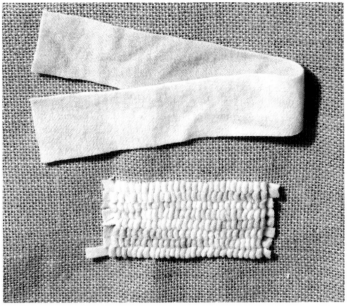

Mottled fabric hooked side-to-side makes a nice sky.

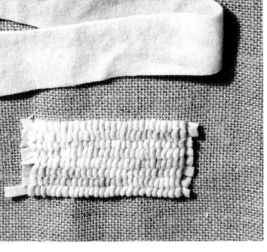

Meandering with mottled wool.

Blocking Your Rug

When you are finished hooking your rug, remove it from the hoop and lay it flat. If it has become out of shape, gently tug it back into shape.

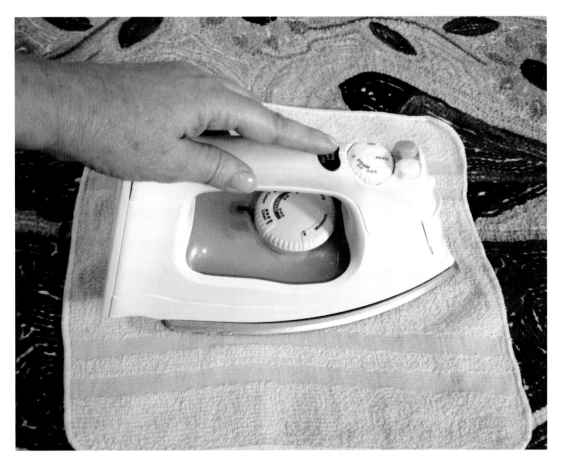

For Blocking your Rug:
Place your rug on an ironing board hooked side up, cover with a damp towel, and place a hot iron on the towel. Don't iron back and forth; instead hold the iron in one section and count to 10. Repeat all over the front of the rug. Flip the rug over and repeat on the back. Let the rug completely dry (usually 24 hours) before finishing the edges.

Finishing Your Rug

There are several methods for finishing the binding of your rug.

Self- Hemming

Zigzag your rug 3" from the hooking and cut away excess backing fabric.

Working from the back, pull the zigzagged edge into the hooking.

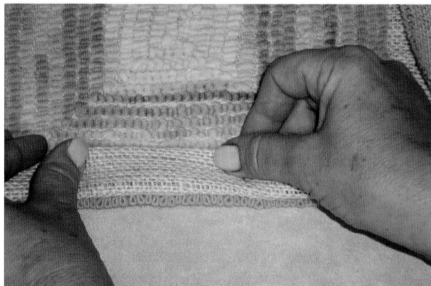

Fold the backing over to back of the rug and blind stitch flat. Make sure your thread goes through the backing fabric.

Zigzag stitch the mitered corner.

Fold to hooked edge.

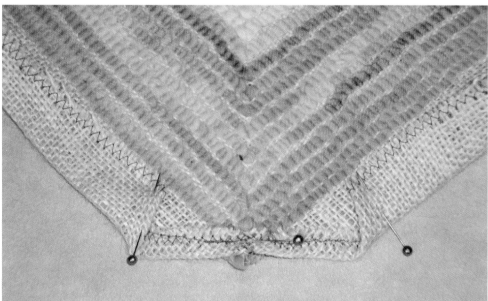

Fold sides to the hooked edge.

Fold the backing to the back of the rug

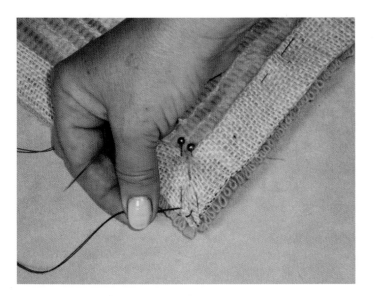

Ready to whipstitch! Start in the corner.

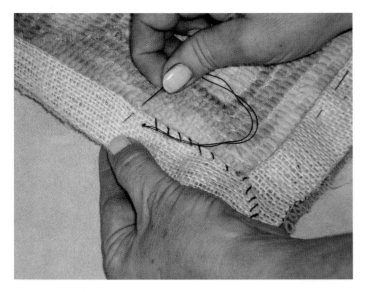

Pull stitch snugly to keep edges together.

Whipstitching with Cording

If you have hooked your rug with wool yarn, use this method.

Mark your backing fabric to 1" from last row of hooking and zigzag on this line. Cut away excess backing. Angle the cuts on the corners.

The cording should be as thick as your rug. Place the rug right side down on a table and place the cording on the outside edge of your hooking.

Flip the rug right side up. Thread a large eyed needle (#16 needlepoint needle) with an 18-24" length of tapestry or wool yarn. Starting in an area that is not on a corner, insert the needle through the back along the hooked edge, pull the yarn through leaving a 2" tail pull the yarn to the back and insert the needle right next to your first stitch catching your tail. You want your first two inches of stitches to cover the tail. When you run out of yarn feed your needle under the already stitched area, bring the needle up and cut off any excess close to the whipstitching.

Continue until you reach the corner. When you reach the corner continue around the edge. You will not have a crisp corner but a slightly rounded one.

Whipstitch flat.

Lay the yarn tail along the cording.

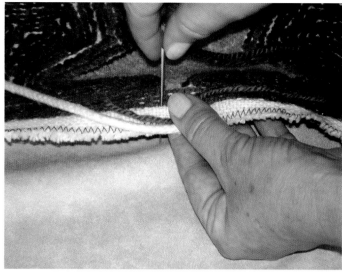

Stick your needle in from the back as close to the hooking as you can.

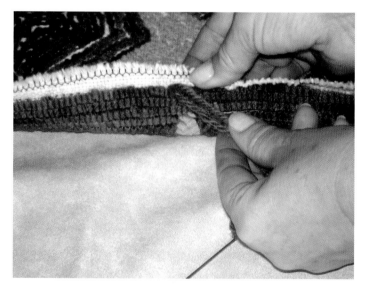

Pull through, leaving two inches of tail along the cording.

Bring the needle over and to the back and stick it in close to the first stitch.

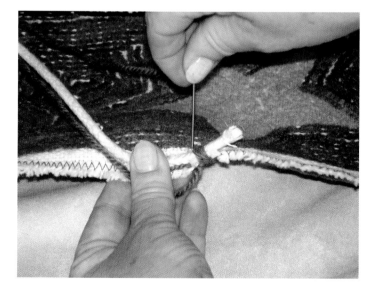

Keep your whipstitching close together.

Finished edge.

Wool with Cording

When purchasing your wool, be sure to buy extra for your edging.

First, zigzag 1" from your hooked edge and cut away excess backing. Then, measure around your rug and add approximately 6". Cut a strip of wool approximately 2 1/2" to 3" in width and the length of your rug plus the 6". It's not necessary to cut on the bias, but it will make it easier to go around the corners. You may need to join together several pieces; join them at right angles, as this reduces bulk.

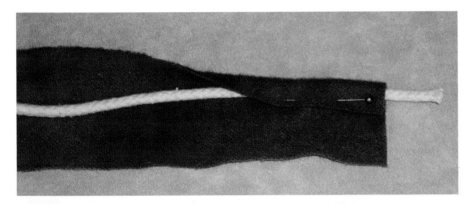

On your long wool strip, place the cording slightly to the right of the center. Fold the left side over the cording.

Using the zipper or cording foot on your sewing machine, sew along the edge of the cording as close as you can. Sew the entire length of the strip with matching thread.

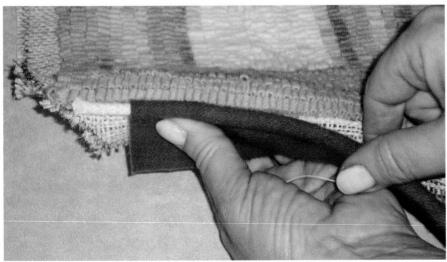

On the front side of the rug, place the stitching line of the wool strip right up against the last row of hooking, leaving the long side free.

For stitching:

- Sew by hand starting about 1" from the edge of the cording. You don't want to see any backing material peeking through on the front.
- When the two edges meet, cut away any excess cording. Fold the raw edge under the piece that will lay on top.
- Miter the corners by folding one edge flat and folding the corner of the other edge on the diagonal. Iron once again using the directions for blocking.

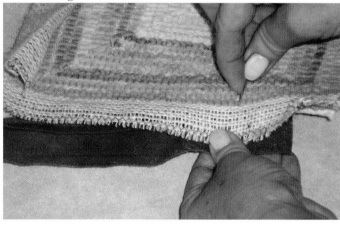

Stick your needle in from the back as close to the hooking as you can.

Come out as close to the sewn seam.

Bring the needle to the back as close to the hooking as you can.

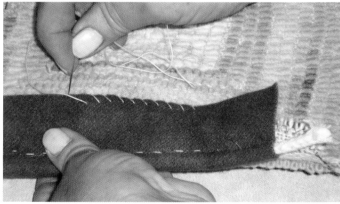

Whipstitch the edge to the backing fabric.

Backing

I don't believe in using latex backing. While doing research for this book, I came across several people and websites that suggest it. When you apply latex to the back of your rug, you are doing several things: preventing air circulation, allowing dirt and sand to stay trapped in and grinding your wool fibers, and making it almost impossible to repair any pulls if they should occur.

If you have hooked correctly, your loops will stay in. To prevent slipping, use a rubber no-slip pad under your rug. You can sew this right to your rug. All of the rugs in my house have no-slip padding sewn on and then they are taped to the floor with a no-slip carpet tape. It peels from the floor when you want to change rugs and leaves no residue.

Blindstitch the non-slip mat to the bottom of your rug.

Hanging Your Rug

Do not tack your rug directly onto your wall. The weight of the wool will pull the corners down and you will damage the rug. The weight needs to be evenly distributed along the top of the rug.

To make your rug into a wall hanging, add a sleeve to the back with wool so that a dowel or rod can be inserted. Whipstitch the sleeve 1" from the top of the back of your project with heavy-duty button thread. Be sure that you sew into the backing fabric and not onto the loops.

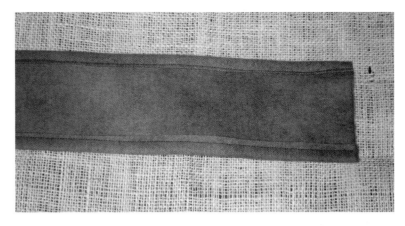

Cut a piece of wool or heavy fabric the width of your project and 4-5" in length. Turn the top and bottom under 1/2" and sew flat. *(Wool doesn't need to be hemmed because it doesn't unravel, but turning it under 1/2" gives you a stronger edge to hold the weight of the rug.)*

Bring the knotted thread through the top of the sleeve.

Bring the needle through to the front along the sleeves stitching line.

Bring the needle up between loops.

Other Hanging Options

Rugs also look wonderful framed like the Fruit in Penny Rug Frame or the Lighthouse Rug Hooking. You can often find frames with wood inserts at local craft stores. If not, or if you hooked your rug before deciding to frame it, just cut a piece of MDF (medium density fiberboard, available at lumber yards) to the finished size of your rug. Place the hooking face down on a table and the MDF board on top, and then staple or tack the excess fabric to the board tightly. Bring this to a frame shop for framing.

Or use foam core board available in craft stores. This is a lightweight material and great if you want to change your piece for the seasons. You can use heavy-duty tape to tape the hooking to the foam core.

The Final Touch

You know many years from now you will never remember when you made your rug or why. On muslin, record your name, the date, and, if there is space, write a few lines — why you made this rug or who you made it for. If you made it as a gift, write the care and cleaning instructions on the label. Write everything with a fine permanent marker. Turn under the edges and blind stitch to the back of your rug.

I make my labels by designing with a scrapbook software program using borders and text. I iron a piece of muslin to the shiny side of an 8 ½" x 11" piece of freezer paper and trim away the excess muslin. I run this through my Desk Jet printer. Cut out the design leaving a 1/2" border, and then turn under the edges and blind stitch to the back of your rug.

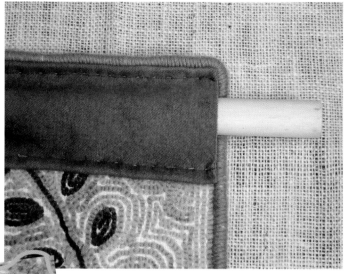

Blind stitch the sleeve to the top of your project and insert a dowel.

From my hands to your heart! Hooked by Christine Jansen November 12, 2008

Computer design on muslin for a rug label.

Care & Cleaning of Your Rug

Your beautiful rug is on the floor and your Siamese likes to sleep on it. How do you remove the cat hair? Some books and websites will tell you not to vacuum. I personally have had no problems vacuuming my rugs. If you choose to vacuum, use a vacuum without a beater roller or brush attachment.

For spills, blot immediately and use a damp cloth with ivory soap gently on that area. Place that area under the faucet and let the stream of water rinse the soap out. Blot dry with a terry cloth towel. Let dry completely before putting it back on the floor to avoid mildew.

When storing rugs, roll them with the hooked side out so that the edges don't curl up.

Chapter Three:
Wool Appliqué

I usually have a wool appliqué project with me wherever I go even if it's just random pennies with no project in mind. I keep different size circles, floss, scissors, and a needle in a makeup bag in my car. When I'm waiting for the kids, for a doctor's appointment, or whatever, I stitch pennies. Later they'll be used for a project such as the Fruit and Pennies Rug on page 56. For other projects, once you have cut out all of your pieces and basted them to your backing, stick your project in the small Hydrangea Craft Folder with sharp scissors, floss, and a needle and your project becomes mobile.

Supplies and Techniques

Wool or Wool Felt

Wool felt can be used in your appliqué projects. It is a blend of wool and rayon. Different brands have different proportions of wool to rayon. Wool felt is less expensive than wool, comes in a variety of colors, and is found in most fabric stores. However, it cannot be used for rug hooking projects and is not as soft as wool.

You can also develop a boiled wool look where the wool will have a raised texture by washing the wool felt. Wet the wool felt, but do not rub or agitate. You will need to wet each color separately as the dye may bleed a bit. Gently squeeze by hand to remove as much water as possible without wringing, as wringing can stretch the material. Dry in the dryer for about 30 minutes, leaving barely damp. Lay flat to dry completely. To remove the boiled wool look, iron with a steam iron.

If using 100% wool, the preparation is the same as for rug hooking. Prewash the wool in hot water and dry it in the dryer.

Freezer Paper

Besides the regular grocery store freezer paper, on the Internet you can find packages of freezer paper that come in 9 ½" x 11", which will go through your home printer.

Wool appliqué supplies featured are woolfelt, needles, needle threader, scissors, floss, and freezer paper.

TIP: Fusible webbing can be used. I don't use this method because I think going through the fusible webbing dulls the needle. If you choose to use fusible webbing, trace the design directly on the webbing, but don't run it through your printer — I've never tried it, but it sounds like a very bad idea. Cut out the shapes and iron onto your main piece of wool according to the fusible web directions.

Floss

Floss is six strands of cotton or linen thread twisted together. You will use three strands for all of these designs unless otherwise indicated. I use DMC floss for my projects, but there are others available. Floss can also be dyed when you dye your wool.

The easiest way to separate the strands is to cut a length of about 18". Not too long because it will tangle and be difficult to pull through your fabric, but not too short because you don't want to keep rethreading your needle. Holding the strand 1" from the cut edge, use your other index finger to tap the cut edge. This will separate the tops of the threads. A purist will separate all six strands and then recombine three of them. I'm not a purist. After tapping, I take three that are close to each other in one hand, the other three in the other hand, and then I VERY SLOWLY pull them apart.

My travel penny pack.

Besides cotton and linen, floss comes in different textures and sheens: *metallic floss* will give sparkle to your projects, *satin floss* has a lustrous sheen, and the *variegated floss* has a mottled look.

Needles and Threader

The needle you use is important. The needles of choice are chenille needles and tapestry needles. Both are sized the same and are very similar. The difference is that the tip of the chenille needle is much sharper than the tapestry needle. Whichever you choose, the eye needs to be large enough to fit the three strands of floss and the tip needs to move smoothly through your wool.

A threader is a great thing to have. Look for the hook style to pull three strands through the eye. The average needle threader is for one strand and won't last with constant use. For convenience, DMC makes a multipurpose threader with three different sides for yarn, medium weight threads, and regular sewing thread.

Clover thread cutter.

Also, a good pair of fabric scissors is invaluable. Do not let anyone else use these scissors to cut anything other than fabric — hide them if you must! Use embroidery scissors for cutting floss.

I fly a lot and hate wasting the time waiting in airports, waiting on the plane for takeoff, and the hours-long flights. I found this pendant cutter by Clover that I put on a chain and wear as a necklace when I fly. Those little grooves cut the threads. I do find that I need a threader when I use this cutter, but it's worth it. I've also used it with crochet yarn and crewel yarn.

Preparing Appliqué

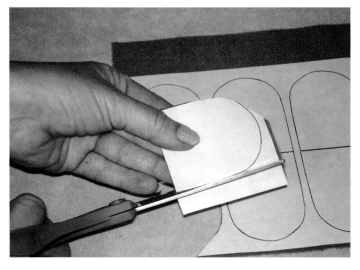

With a dry iron, press the freezer paper (shiny side down) onto the wool.

Enlarge your pattern to the appropriate size and either hand trace it or run it through the printer onto the dull side of the freezer paper. Cut out the individual pieces and lay them on the correct color of wool; be sure to group them close to each other to conserve wool.

Cut out all of the pieces. I use my Sizzix machine to cut out my pennies and other shapes I use in wool appliqué. I can double the wool and cut out two at once.

Remove freezer paper.

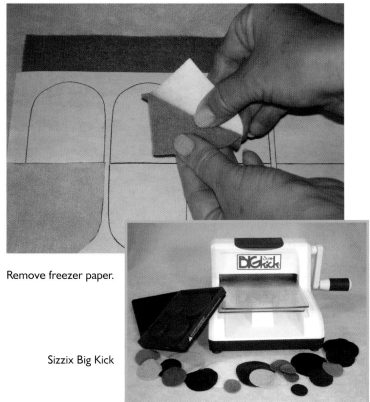

Sizzix Big Kick

Arrange your cut pieces onto your main piece according to the picture. Baste all of the pieces in place by hand. Basting is sewing with loose temporary stitches. These will be easy to pull out with a needle when you are through. It also makes your project more portable because everything stays in place.

Baste pieces to backing.

Stitching

There are so many really great stitches. I'm going to cover the ones I use in my designs. Other stitches can be found in crazy quilt and needlework books.

Blanket stitch

Bring needle from back.

Catch bottom fabric and top fabric.

Pull through, leaving a loop.

Run needle through loop.

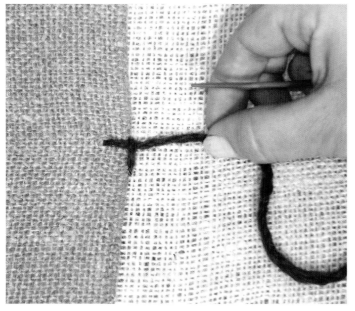

Pull gently to tighten.

Run needle through next loop.

Repeat first step.

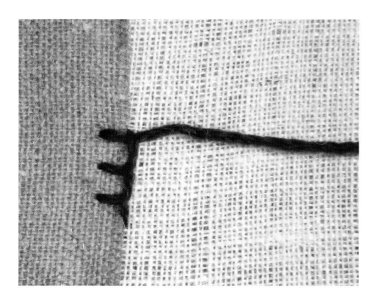

Pull to tighten.

Repeat...making nice even stitches.

Chain Stitch

Bring needle from back.

From the top, place the needle in close to where you pulled it up.

Pull the thread until you have a small loop with the loose thread inside the loop.

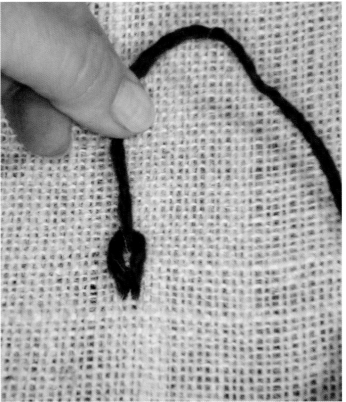

Pull the thread to finish the chain stitch.

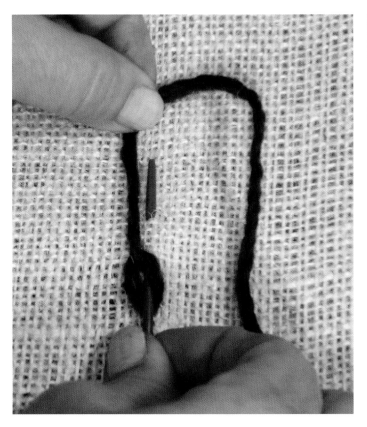

Place the needle in close to where it came out; the top of the needle should be the same distance as your first stitch.

With thread inside of loop, pull gently to tighten.

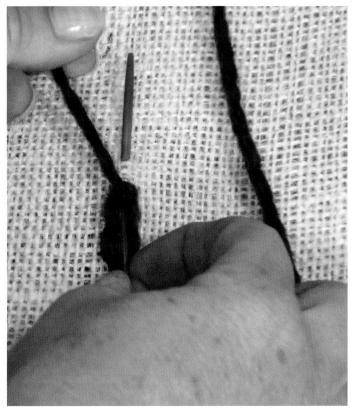

Repeat.

Nice line of chain stitches.

Fern Stitch

I learned the Fern stitch on my own from seeing it on a crazy quilt. I didn't know what the stitch was called, so I looked it up in a needlework book. In the book, they begin at the top and work towards the bottom. When I do it, I start at the bottom and work upwards. The results are the same, so do some practice stitches to see which way works for you.

Bring needle from back.

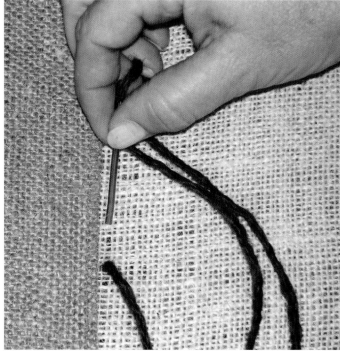

Stick the needle into the fabric approximately 1/2" up.

Pull the thread to make first stitch.

Bring the needle up in the same hole as the beginning stitch.

44

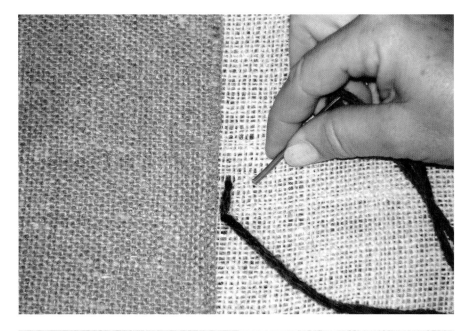

Put the needle in to the right of the first stitch.

Pull gently.

Bring needle up in the same place as the first step.

45

Place the needle in to the left of the first stitch.

First stitch is finished.

Bring the needle up in the same hole as the first stitch went in to continue making a border.

Continue on with the fern stitch.

Labels

I can't emphasize enough to sign and date things. It's a great way to compare when you started to how you have progressed. I use labels on my wool appliqué as well as my rug hooking. I follow the same technique as with the rug hooking labels, but you can sew the labels on the back piece with your sewing machine before you attach the front piece to the back piece.

Chapter Four:
Rug Projects

NOTE: The patterns for all the projects appear in the "Patterns" section of the Appendix.

Welcome Thyme Hooked Rug

Finished size: 17 1/2" x 29"
#5 Cut

Material

Wool

- 1/2 yard: Various Blues
- 1/4 yard: Green
- 10" x 8": Gold
- 16" x 6": Red
- 10" x 6": Brown
- 10" x 5": Black
- 10" x 3": Yellow
- 10" x 2": White
- 10" x 2": Dark Brown
- 6" x 2": Mottled Brown

Other Supplies

- 24" x 37": Backing Fabric
- 4 oz.: Skein blue wool yarn for binding
- 2 oz.: Skein brown wool for binding
- 10'5": Cording

Welcome Thyme on red dot tracer.

Transferring and Hooking the Pattern

Enlarge the pattern and transfer onto your backing fabric. Refer to "Transferring Your Pattern" in Chapter Two. Finish the edges, referring to "Finishing the Edges" also in Chapter Two.

Hook the rug in the following order:

- Roof, windows, and doorknob: Black
- Shutters: Yellow
- Door: Mottled brown
- House and chimney: Red
- Smoke: White
- Tree trunks: Dark Brown
- Leaves: Green
- "Welcome": Gold
- Background: Blues
- Ground: Brown

Block your rug, referring to "Blocking Your Rug" in Chapter Two.

Finish the rug following "Whipstitching with Cording" or any of the other options in the "Finishing Your Rug" section in Chapter Two.

Block again following "Blocking Your Rug."

Fruit Rug Hooking

Finished size: 12 ½" x 7"
#5 Cut

Material

Wool

- 15" X 10" Light Blue
- 12" x 10" Medium Green
- 10" x 6" Dark Purple
- 10" x 6" Medium Purple
- 10" x 6" Light Purple
- 8" x 8" Yellow
- 6" x 6" Light Green
- 6" x 6" Red
- 6" x 2" Dark Green
- Scrap dark brown
- 20" x 15" Backing fabric

Transferring and Hooking the Pattern

Enlarge the pattern and transfer onto your backing fabric. Finish the edges with a zigzag stitch to prevent unraveling referring to the techniques section.

Hook the rug in the following order:

- Pear: Yellow
- Apple: Red
- Stems: Brown
- Veins on large leaves: Dark Green
- Large leaves: Medium Green
- Small leaves: Light Green
- Grapes: Dark, Medium, and Light Purples
- Background: Light Blue

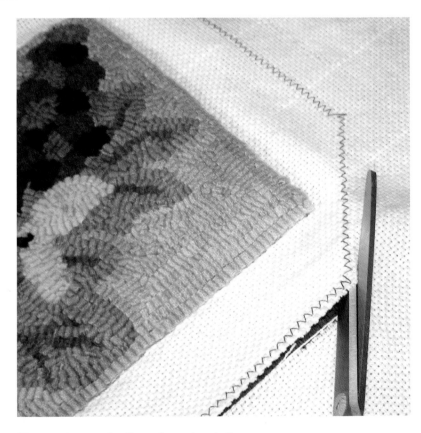

Zigzag 2" from the edge of hooking. *I sewed on the diagonal towards the corners to reduce bulk on the backside.*

Block your rug following "Blocking Your Rug" in Chapter Two, and secure to the back of the insert board with staples or heavy-duty tape.

Zigzag and cut on the diagonal to reduce bulk.

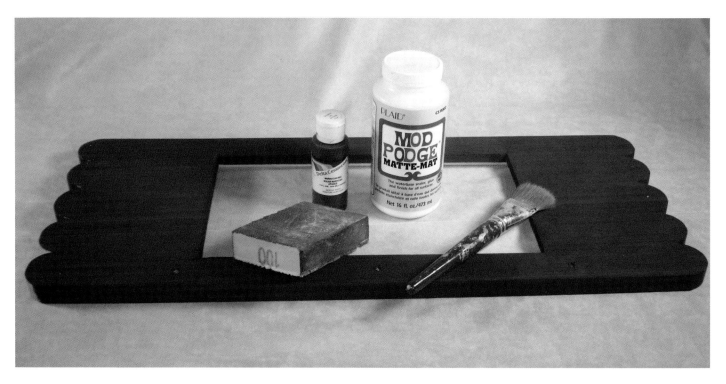

Featured is a Wool Penny frame, along with supplies that include sandpaper, paint, sealer, and a paint brush.

Wood Penny Frame

Decoart Americana 2 oz. Paints:
- Antique Gold
- Baby Blue
- Black Plum
- Crimson Tide
- Dark Chocolate
- Raw Sienna
- Uniform Blue
- Williamsburg Blue

Other Supplies
- Penny rug frame with insert *(see Resources)*
- Mod Podge
- Foam dinner plate or clean meat tray
- Small piece of card stock (heavy paper)
- Medium sandpaper
- Ruler
- Chalk pencil
- 1" Loew Cornell Wash brush
- Size 10 Loew Cornell Flat brush
- Size 18/0 Loew Cornell Liner brush (very skinny)
- Bowl for water
- Paper towels
- Craft varnish
- Sawtooth picture hanger

To basecoat, pour a puddle of paint onto a foam plate. Load the brush evenly by brushing it back and forth in the puddle; do not overload the brush. Apply the paint in long brush strokes back and forth on the surface including the inside and outside edges. It's important to do thin, even strokes. Heavy strokes will leave ridges. A good, smooth basecoat will give you a better-looking project when finished.

Seal the wood frame with a coat of Mod Podge — the front and all of the edges. Don't forget the little pegs. Let dry. You do not have to do the back or the insert. Lightly sand to remove any roughness. Basecoat the front, the inside and outside edges, and the pegs with Crimson Tide. Let dry. *(Note: Red can be a tough color to basecoat, as it often takes three or four coats. Let dry between each coat.)*

Mark off 2" on each side of the opening with a chalk pencil. Trace the tongue pattern onto the heavy card stock and cut out. Trace on the tongues with the chalk pencil. Basecoat each one with Antique Gold. This may take three coats; let each coat dry thoroughly before continuing.

Dip brush into the water.

For Shading:

Add shading with Burnt Sienna using the #10 flat brush. Pour out a quarter size puddle of shading color onto your palette (can be either a foam plate or meat tray).

Trace the circle pattern onto the heavy card stock and cut out. Draw on circles using the template. Basecoat with Baby Blue. Add shading with Williamsburg Blue using the #10 flat brush. Shade the areas of red with Black Plum where indicated on the pattern.

The stitching is done using the liner brush. When using a liner brush, pour out a puddle of paint and thin with a little water to an inky consistency. Pull the liner through the thinned paint and make a stroke on the foam plate to remove any excess. The stitches are just small strokes: Black Plum on the Crimson Red, Dark Chocolate on the Antique Gold, and Uniform Blue on the Baby Blue.

Let the frame dry for 24 hours. Apply two thin coats of varnish. Let dry.

Secure the insert into the frame, add the picture hanger, and you are done!

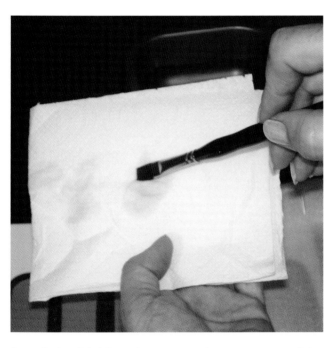

Press the brush lightly on the paper towel to remove some of the water. Be sure to still retain some water.

Dip one corner of the tip of the brush into the paint.

On your paint palette, move your brush back and forth in the same spot, working the paint into one side of the brush and letting it fade out on the other side.

Stroke the loaded brush with the painted edge along the outside of where you want to shade.

Wait until the shading is dry on one side to start the other side.

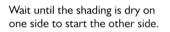

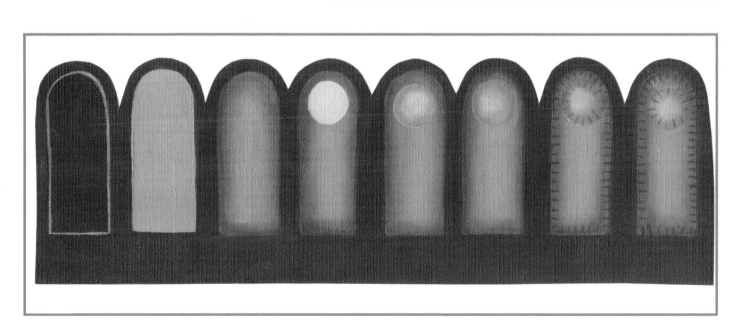

Stages of painting the frame.

Fruit Penny Rug

Finished size: 18" x 15"

Materials

Choose your floss to coordinate with your wool. Try to get one or two shades darker. The floss colors listed are the ones I used in this project. Use up scraps of wool to make the pennies.

Wool or Wool Felt
- 1/3 yard: Black
- 15" x 10": Light Blue
- 12" x 10": Medium Green
- 10" x 6": Dark Purple
- 10" x 6": Medium Purple
- 10" x 6": Light Purple
- 8" x 8": Yellow
- 6" x 6": Light Green
- 6" x 6": Red
- 6" x 2": Dark Green
- 1/4 yard various colors for pennies

DMC Floss
- 221 Shell Pink, Very Dark
- 333 Blue Violet, Very Dark
- 581 Moss Green
- 839 Beige Brown, Dark
- 937 Avocado Green, Medium
- 977 Golden Brown, Light

Other Supplies
- Chalk or chalk pencil
- Basting thread
- Chenille or tapestry needle

Transferring and Hooking the Pattern

Enlarge the pattern and transfer onto freezer paper. Then cut 17" x 11" for the back in brown, 17" x 6" in blue, and 17" x 5" in brown

After ironing onto the appropriate wool/wool felt, cut:

- One oval: Light Blue
- Large leaves: Medium Green
- Apple: Red
- Pear: Yellow
- 36 circles for the grapes: Purples

Using the photo as a diagram, place everything except the grapes on the oval, but leave enough room to add the grapes in later. Baste everything into place.

Stitching

All stitching is done with three strands of floss.

- Large leaves first with 937 Avocado Green Medium using a blanket stitch; then using the same color, chain stitch the veins.
- Pear with 977 Golden Brown Light using a blanket stitch; then using the same color, chain stitch a little dimple in the top.
- Apple 221 Shell Pink Very Dark using a blanket stitch; then using the same color, chain stitch a little dimple in the top.
- Stems: chain stitch with six strands of 839 Beige Brown Dark.
- Small leaves with 581 Moss Green using a blanket stitch; then using the same color, chain stitch the veins.
- Baste on the grapes in clusters and blanket stitch with 333 Blue Violet Very Dark all of the areas of the grapes that are showing. With 977 Golden Brown Light, chain stitch small stems to some of the grapes and stems at the top of each cluster.
- Remove all basting stitches and press with a hot iron from the backside.
- Make 17 pennies of various colors using up any leftover scraps. To make the pennies, blanket stitch the smallest penny to the medium penny and the medium penny to the large penny; it can be your choice of colors.

Center the blue oval on the black rectangle.

Arrange the pennies around the edge of the oval. Keep rearranging until you're happy with the colors. Run a long basting stitch through the centers of the pennies to secure them to the blue and black, and then baste the outside edges of the pennies to the black.

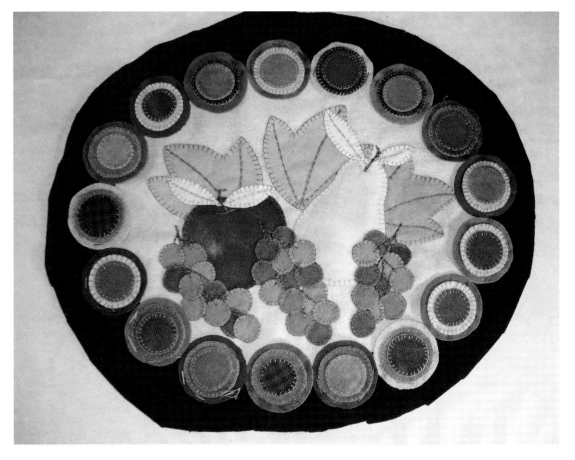

Roughly cut a large oval to reduce the bulk while you are doing the blanket stitching. Blanket stitch each individual penny using various floss colors.

Chalk a 1/2" scallop around the outside of pennies.

Sandwich the other black square and baste around the outside of the pennies. I ran a large baste stitch crosswise through the entire sandwich to keep it from shifting. (I do a lot of basting because it keeps my projects portable.)

Cut on scalloped line.

To Finish: Blanket stitch with various colors of floss, remove basting stitches, press on the backside with a steam iron, and press the front using a pressing cloth on top of the wool.

Wool appliqué in frame.

This project can also be done the same size as the Fruit Rug Hooking without the pennies and framed in the wooden frame.

Pennies from Heaven Rug

Finished size: 39" x 12"
#5 Cut (or whatever strips you
want to use up)

This project is a great way to use up leftover strips (and/or yarn)! Or you can pick colors to coordinate with your décor. You can also make it large and wider and use it as a floor runner.

Materials

Wool
- 1/2 yard: Various Colors
- 1/3 yard: Background color

Other Supplies
- 47" x 20": Backing fabric
- 4 oz. Skein wool yarn for binding
- 9'5" cording

Transferring and Hooking the Pattern

Enlarge the pattern and transfer onto your backing fabric. Refer to "Transferring Your Pattern." Finish the edges referring to "Finishing the Edges." *(Both in Chapter Two.)*

Hook the rug starting in the center and working outwards. Make sure you vary your "penny" colors. Hook the background as you go.

Block your rug *(refer to "Blocking Your Rug")* and finish the rug referring to "Whipstitching with Cording" or any of the other options in the Finishing Your Rug section.

Block again, referring to "Blocking Your Rug."

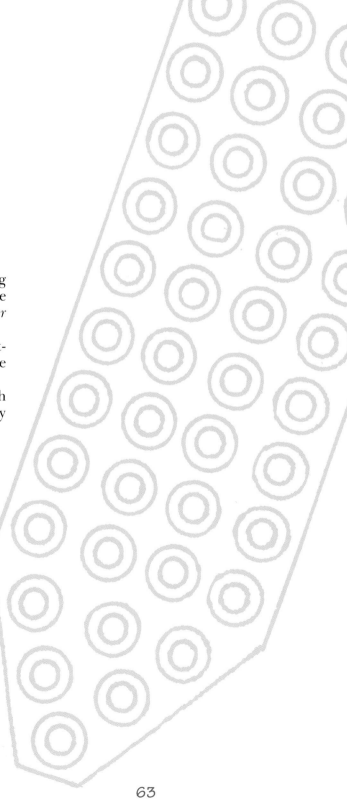

Crows on Watermelon
Hooked Rug

Finished size: 24" x 36"
#5 Cut

Materials

Wool
- 1/2 yard various blues
- 1/3 yard white
- 1/3 yard black
- 16" x 16" Red
- 10" x 6" Yellow
- 10" x 6" Brown
- 10" x 5" Green
- 10" x 4" Gold
- 10" x 4" Orange
- 10" x 3" Grey

Other Supplies
- 32" x 44" Backing Fabric
- 4 oz. Skein black wool yarn for binding
- 10'5" Cording

Transferring and Hooking the Pattern

Enlarge the pattern and transfer onto your backing fabric. Refer to "Transferring Your Pattern." Finish the edges referring to "Finishing the Edges."

Hook the rug in the following order:

- Flower centers: Brown
- Back petals: Gold
- Front petals, crows' eye, and beak: Yellow
- Crow body: Grey
- Crow leg, tail, claws, and head: Black
- Watermelon seeds: Black
- Wings: Orange
- Watermelon flesh: Red
- Watermelon white rind: White
- Rind and leaves: Green
- Ground and vines: Brown
- Sky: Blues

The border diamond pattern is hooked in black and white.

Block your rug *(refer to "Blocking Your Rug")* and finish the rug referring to "Whipstitching with Cording" or any of the other options in the Finishing Your Rug section.

Block again, referring to "Blocking Your Rug."

Crows on Watermelon
Wool Appliqué

Finished size: 21" x 15"

Materials

Wool or Wool Felt

- 1/2-yard brown
- 17" x 6" Blue
- 17" x 5" Red
- 17" x 5" Green
- 16" x 8" White
- 14" x 14" Black
- 8" x 8" Grey
- 8" x 8" Orange
- 8" x 6" Yellow
- 6" x 6" Orange

DMC Floss

I used floss colors that coordinated with my wool. Bring swatches of your wool and purchase your floss one shade darker.

- Blanc (2)
- 247 Salmon, Very dark
- 310 Black
- 434 Brown, Light
- 500 Blue Green, Very Dark
- 676 Old Gold, Light
- 920 Copper, Medium
- 3799 Pewter Gray, Very Dark

Other Supplies

- White seed beads 10/0
- 22 3mm white beads
- Beading needle
- 9 black buttons
- 20" white ric rac
- White thread

Transferring and Hooking the Pattern

Enlarge pattern and transfer onto freezer paper. Then cut 17" x 11" for the back in brown, 17" x 6" in blue, and 17" x 5" in brown

After ironing onto the appropriate wool/wool felt, cut:

- Watermelon flesh: Red
- Watermelon rind, 6 leaves: Green
- Wings: Orange
- Tail, head, front legs, 52 tongues: Black
- Back legs, upper tail (rear end): Grey
- 20 small petals, 8 large: Yellow
- 20 small petals, 8 large: Gold
- 26 pennies: White
- 1 large flower center, 2 ½ small centers: Brown

NOTE: For the next steps, when you finish an area that has been basted, remove basting stitches before going onto the next section.

Slightly overlap blue sky onto brown (17" x 5") bottom and baste. This is the front piece that all your other pieces will go on.

Place watermelon flesh and rind on the front piece. Blanket stitch the top edge of the watermelon flesh with 347 Salmon Very Dark and tack the lower edge to keep in place. Baste on the rind bottom edge and blanket stitch with 500 Blue Green Very Dark. Place on the ric rac and secure with a running stitch using white thread. With 434 Brown Light, make running stitch rows on the brown wool under the watermelon. Sew on the nine black buttons with white thread.

Lay out both bird pieces and baste into place. Beaks are blanket stitched with 676 Old Gold Light. Head, front leg, and tail are blanket stitched with 310 Black. Gray body parts are blanket stitched with 3799 Pewter Gray Very Dark. Stitch a running stitch for the legs. The wings are blanket stitched with 920 Copper Medium. Curvy stitches are a running stitch of 920 Copper Medium.

Place on the sunflowers and baste into place. The center and back petals are blanket stitched with 434 Brown Light. Top sunflower petals are blanket stitched with 676 Old Gold Light. For the three smaller sunflowers, sew on the seed beads using the beading needle and white thread. For the large sunflower, sew on the 3mm beads using white thread.

Blanket stitch leaves into place with 500 Blue Green Very Dark. Make the center vein by chain stitching. Then chain stitch the brown vine using 434 Brown Light.

Attach a white penny to a black tongue with 310 Black using a blanket stitch. Attach the black tongue with Blanc using a blanket stitch. Baste or pin the tongues to the front finished piece and baste on the back brown piece. Blanket stitch with 310 Black to secure the three layers together and press gently from the backside.

Lighthouse Framed Rug Hooking

Finished Size: 8"
#5 Cut

Materials

Wool
- 10" x 10" Light Blue
- 10" x 6" Green
- 10" x 6" White
- 10" x 6" Red
- 6" x 6" Black
- 6" x 6" Beige
- Scrap of Yellow or Gold

Other Supplies
- 20" x 15" backing fabric
- Frame
- Foam core

I found this frame at a discount store. It had a mirror in it, which I removed. I then traced the inside onto a piece of foam core board to mount the rug hooking on.

Transferring and Hooking the Pattern

Enlarge pattern and transfer onto your backing fabric. Finish the edges with a zigzag stitch to prevent unraveling *(refer to techniques section in Chapter Two)*.

~ Hook in the following order:

- Windows: Black
- Doors: Red
- Lighthouse, house on left, front of house on right, and clouds: White
- Far left house and side of right house: Beige
- Roofs: Red
- Light: Yellow or Gold
- Railing: Black
- Lighthouse roof: Red
- Sky: Blue
- Ground: Green

Zigzag 2" from the edge of hooking and block your rug following the instructions in Chapter Two.

Doing the Frame

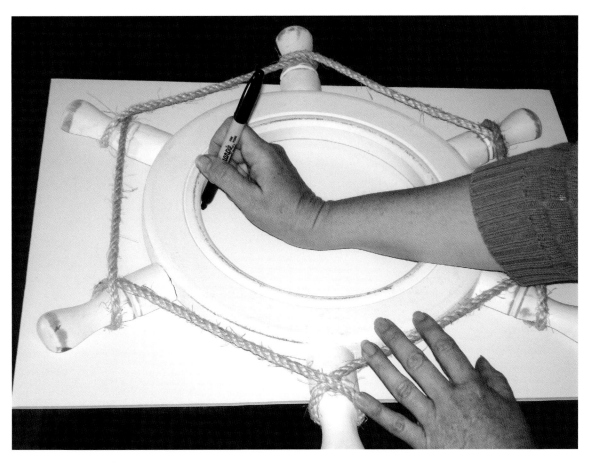

If your frame didn't come with an insert, cut a piece of foam core using the frame as a guide.

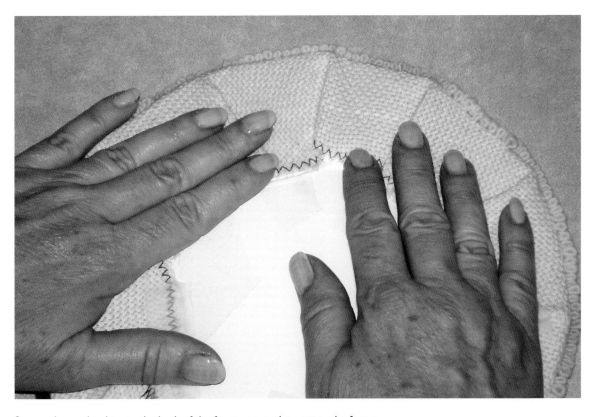

Secure the rug hooking to the back of the foam core and mount to the frame.

Lighthouse Penny Rug

Finished size:
14" diameter

Materials

Wool
- 1/2-yard White
- 14" x 14" Light Blue
- 10" x 6" White
- 10" x 6" Red
- 6" x 4" Green
- Scrap of Yellow or Gold
- Scrap of Black

DMC Floss
- Blanc
- 310 Black (3)
- 744 Yellow, Pale
- 3345 Hunter Green, Dark

Other Supplies:
- Chalk or chalk pencil
- Basting thread
- Chenille or tapestry needle
- 32" of 1/4" rope-like trim or cording

Transferring and Hooking the Project

Enlarge pattern. Transfer onto freezer paper.

Cut out an 8" circle from the light blue.
After ironing onto the appropriate wool/wool felt, cut:

- Lighthouse, houses, clouds, and medium pennies: White
- Roofs, doors, and small pennies: Red
- Land: Green
- Large pennies: Light blue
- Windows: Black

Using the photo as a diagram, place everything on the light blue circle. Baste everything in place and stitch:

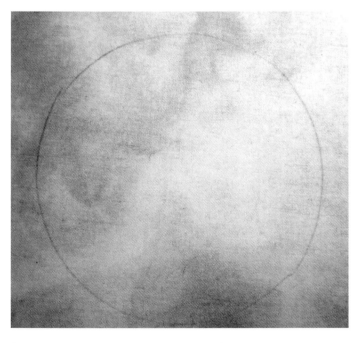

Draw your circle on an interesting section of the wool.

Blanket stitch:
- Lighthouse, houses, windows, and clouds: Blanc
- Roofs and doors: 310 Black
- Grass: 3345 Hunter Green, Dark

Chain stitch:
- Walkway: 310 Black
- Light beams: 744 Yellow, Pale

Remove all basting stitches and press with a hot iron from the backside.

To make the pennies, blanket stitch the smallest penny to the medium penny and the medium penny to the large penny with 310 Black.

Center the blue oval on the white square. Arrange the pennies around the edge of the circle. You may have to "shave" some of the pennies to make them fit. Run a long basting stitch through the centers of the pennies to secure them to the blue and black. Baste the outside edges of the pennies to the white.

Chalk a 1/2" scallop around the outside of pennies. Cut on scalloped line. Blanket stitch the pennies using 310 Black.

Sew trim around center with 310 Black using a loose whipstitch.

Sandwich the other white square and baste around the outside of the pennies. Cut using the top scalloped edge as a pattern. Blanket stitch with 310 Black.

Remove basting stitches. Press on the backside with a steam iron.

Lay the top on the back and pin.

"Loden" Hooked Rug

Finished size: 50" x 34"
#5 Cut

In my last book, I had a lot of pictures of my Westie, Dooney. This rug is of my beautiful dog, Loden. He is a German Shorthair Pointer with large and small patches of dark brown (liver) and white. We nicknamed him Velcro because he always "sticks" close by.

The border is a great way to use up scraps and excess strands from other projects. I did this rug in yarn, but the instructions are for wool strips. Use this pattern as a jumping off point to hook your favorite dog. Make the tail longer, the ears shorter, and the coloring your own.

Materials

Wool
- 1/2-yard Light Blue
- 1/2-yard Medium Blue
- 1/4-yard Dark brown
- 1/8-yard Greens
- 6" x 4" Black
- 1-yard scraps and remainders

Other Supplies
- 58" x 42" backing fabric
- 10 feet of cording
- 4 oz. yarn for binding

Transferring and Hooking the Rug

Enlarge pattern and transfer onto your backing fabric. Finish the edges with a zigzag stitch to prevent unraveling *(refer to techniques section in Chapter Two)*.

I did the patches first. To get the brindled look for the rest of his fur, I pulled a strand of dark brown and a strand of white up through the same hole.

Hook the rug in the following order:

- Eye and Mouth: Black (make a small highlight in the eye of white)
- Body: Dark Brown and White
- Grass: Greens
- Sky: Meander *(see page 26)* with medium and light blues
- Border: Make each square a different color using your scrap wools

Zigzag 1/2" from the edge of hooking.
Block your rug *(refer to "Blocking Your Rug")* and finish the rug referring to "Whipstitching with Cording" or any of the other options in the Finishing Your Rug section.
Block again, referring to "Blocking Your Rug."

Two tails in one hole.

Two loops in one hole.

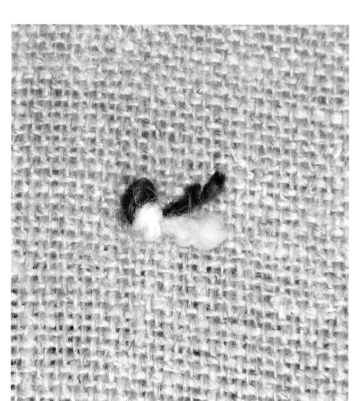

Continue bringing up two loops in one hole
for a brindled look.

Facial detail.

Pineapple Rug Hooking

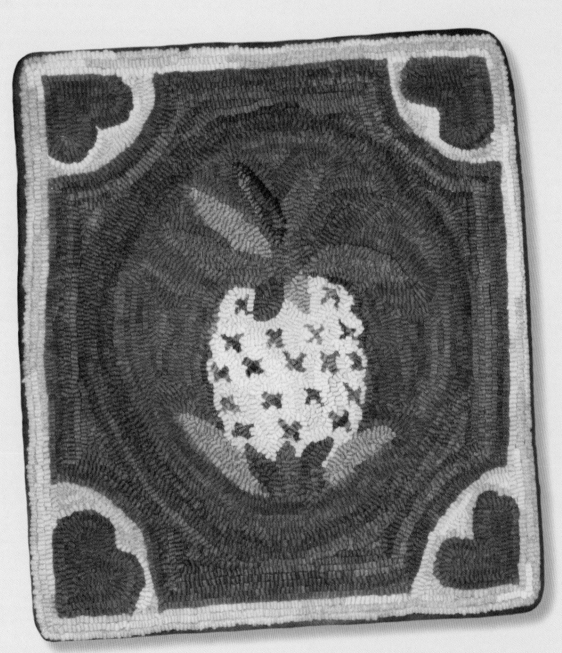

Finished size: 16" x 14"
#5 Cut

Materials

Wool
- 1/4-yard various greens
- 14" x 14" various oranges plus 60" x 3" wool for binding
- 14" x 14" Various Yellows
- 6" x 2" Brown

Other Supplies:
- 24" x 22" Backing fabric
- 5' Cording

Transferring and Hooking the Rug

Enlarge pattern and transfer onto your backing fabric. Finish the edges with a zigzag stitch to prevent unraveling *(refer to techniques section in Chapter Two)*.

Hook the rug in the following order:

- Outline of Pineapple and "X's": Brown
- Pineapple: Various Yellows
- Leaves: Each in a different green
- Orange circle: Various Oranges
- Green frame: Various Greens
- Outline and corner hearts: Various Oranges
- Background: Various Yellows

Zigzag 2" from the edge of hooking.

Block your rug *(refer to "Blocking Your Rug")* and finish the rug referring to "Whipstitching with Cording" or any of the other options in the Finishing Your Rug section.

Pineapple Heart Wool Appliqué

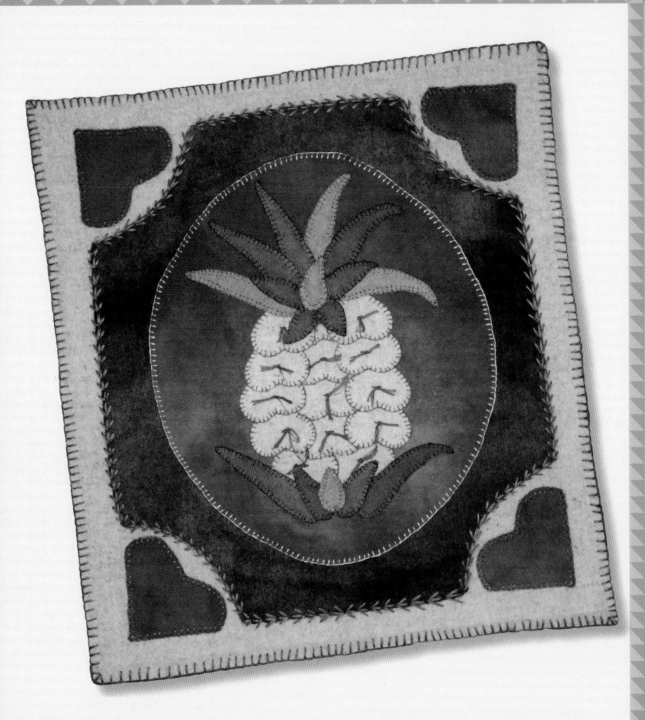

Finished size: 16" x 15"

Materials

Wool

- (2) 16" x 15" pieces of Gold
- 14" x 13" Green
- 14" x 14" Various Oranges
- 10" x 10" Gold
- 8" x 8" Various Greens

DMC Floss

- 310 Black
- 500 Blue Green, Very Dark
- 676 Old Gold, Light
- 720 Orange Spice, Dark
- 920 Copper, Medium
- 921 Copper
- 975 Golden Brown, Dark
- 977 Golden Brown, Light
- 3847 Teal Green, Dark

Transferring and Hooking the Rug

Enlarge pattern. Transfer onto freezer paper. After ironing onto the appropriate wool/wool felt, cut:

- 14 Small Hearts: Gold
- Leaves: Various Greens
- Oval: Orange
- Inner Frame: Green
- 4 Large Hearts: Orange

Layer the hearts into a pineapple shape on the orange oval. Baste into place. With three strands of 975 Golden Brown Dark, blanket stitch around visible portions of hearts. With 6 strands of 975 Golden Brown Dark, make a knot in the center of each heart, leaving about 3/4" tails.

Refer to the pattern for crown placement. Baste all leaves into place. Blanket stitch around the visible portions of the leaves. For the darker leaves, use 2 strands of 310 Black and 1 strand of 500 Blue Green Very Dark. For mid color leaves, sew with 1 strand of 310 Black and 2 strands of 500 Blue Green Very Dark. The lightest leaves are blanket stitched with 3 strands of 3847 Teal Green Dark. Do the same with the bottom leaves.

Lay the orange oval on the green frame shape, baste, and blanket stitch with 676 Old Gold Light.

Lay the green frame onto the 16" x 15" gold piece. Using the Fern stitch from *Chapter Three* and 2 strands 921 Copper, 2 strands 720 Orange Spice Dark, and 2 strands 920 Copper Medium (6 strands altogether), attach the green to the gold. *NOTE: The Fern stitch starts in the middle of the bottom and goes to the middle of the top in one direction and then in the other direction on the other side.*

Baste the larger hearts in place and blanket stitch with 2 strands 3847 Teal Green Dark and 1 strand of 500 Blue Green Very Dark. Then attach the front panel to the back and blanket stitch together using 6 strands of 975 Golden Brown Dark.

Remove any remaining basting stitches and press with a hot iron from the backside.

Chapter Five:
Other Fun Projects

Hydrangea Rug Hooked Pillow

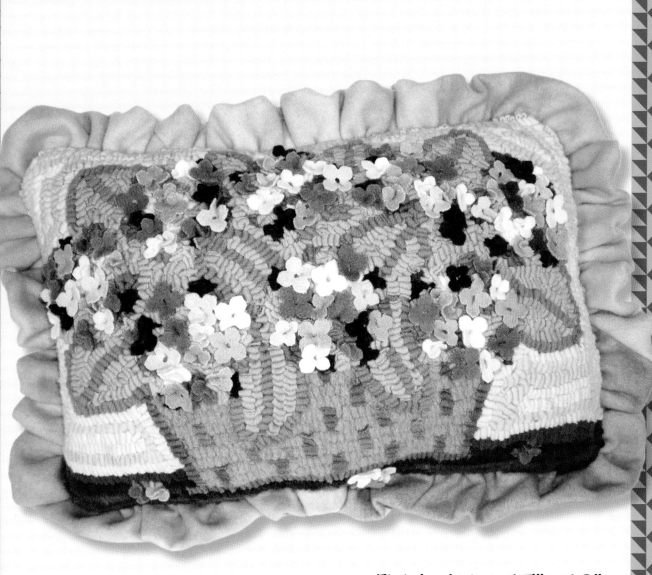

Finished size: 17" x 12"
#8 Cut

Materials

You can make the ruffle and backing with fabric instead of wool. A nice blue and yellow toile would be nice with these colors.

Wool

- 12" x 12" Blues
- 12" x 12" Light Green
- 10" x 6" Yellows
- 10" x 6" White
- 8" x 6" Dark Green
- 8" x 6" Dark Brown
- 8" x 6" Golds
- 6" x 4" Brown
- Extra wool or regular fabric for ruffle
(2 yards) and back (15" x 10")

Other Supplies

- 25" x 20" backing fabric
- Heavy duty button thread
- Fiberfill

Bring up clusters of loops to make petals.

Transferring and Hooking the Pillow

Enlarge pattern and transfer onto your backing fabric. Finish the edges with a zigzag stitch to prevent unraveling (*refer to techniques section in Chapter Two*). Hook in the following order:

- Basket Spokes: Brown
- Basket Weave: Gold
- Leaves: Outline in Dark Green and fill in with Light Green
- Petals: Blues and White
- Table (lower portion): Dark Browns
- Background: Various Yellows

Zigzag 1" from the edge of hooking and block your rug following "Blocking Your Rug." Then cut out approximately 60 petals. Attach to the petal area with rug thread.

To make the ruffle:

Cut a strip of fabric 4" x 2" yards. Fold in half lengthwise and iron flat. With a loose running stitch and the button thread, stitch along the open edge gathering both thickness of fabric. Pull the thread slowly making the ruffle, easing the thread gently. Pin securely, adjusting the gathers so the fullness is distributed evenly.

Place the ruffle along the hooked edge with the ruffle towards the center of the pillow. Pin securely. Stitch the ruffle to the hooked area as close to the hooking as possible.

To Finish:

Sandwich the front to the back (right sides together) and pin. Again, sew as close to the hooking as possible, leaving a good size opening to invert. Use a very sharp needle, as the sandwich will be very thick.

Turn the pillow inside out; it will be a little difficult because the hooked area isn't very flexible. Push out the corners. Insert fiberfill and whipstitch the opening closed.

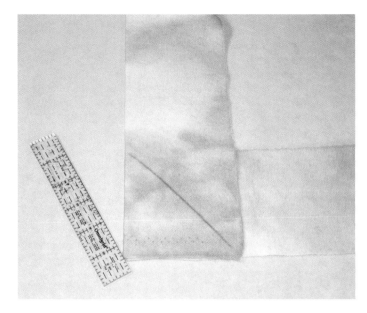

Lay two pieces perpendicular. Make a line corner to corner.

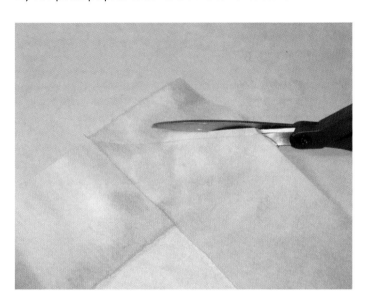

Cut away excess after sewing.

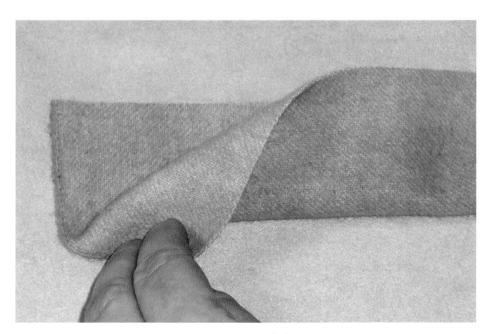

Fold strip in half.

85

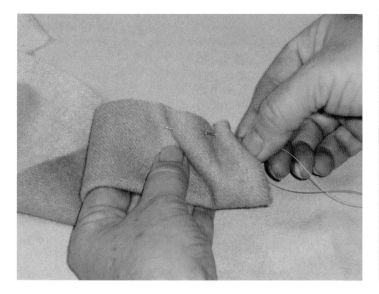

Run a gathering stitch.

Pull the thread to gather the ruffle.

Pin the ruffle to the hooked side.

Stitch as close to the hooking as possible.

Hydrangea Make-do

Materials

Wool
- 1/4-yard Medium Blue
- 10" x 10" Green
- 6" x 6" Light Blue
- 6" x 6" Dark Blue
- 6" x 6" White

Other Supplies
- Blue thread
- Candlestick
- Green floss (3345 Hunter Green Dark)
- Fiberfill
- Tacky glue

The Project

Cut out 6 ball pieces, 10 leaf pieces, and approximately 150 petal pieces. The petal pieces are easy to do with the Sizzix Big Shot.

Whipstitch together by sewing from one end to 2" from the other end.

Keep adding pieces and repeat until they are all joined.

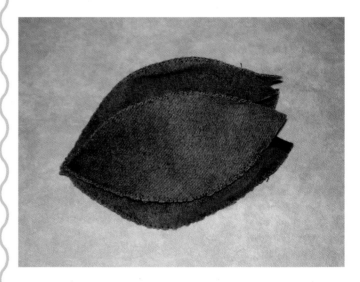

The form should resemble a squid!

Invert the ball and attach petals ending approximately 2" from the bottom... Now it's a jelly fish!

Through the hole.

Into the petal.

Leave approximately 2".

Push the ends to the inside and sew a gathering (loose running) stitch catching both layers of wool.

Stuff the inside with fiberfill and pull the thread to gather the bottom until it fits over your candlestick. Chain stitch 5 leaves with veins with dark green floss. Blanket stitch each top leaf to a bottom (unstitched) leaf with dark green floss.

Attach three leaves to the bottom of the hydrangea and glue the hydrangea to the candlestick to secure. Glue 2 leaves to the base of the candlestick.

Hydrangea Rug Hook Tool

Materials

Decoart Americana 2 oz. colors:
- Hauser Dark Green
- Hauser Light Green
- Hauser Medium Green
- Sapphire Blue
- Snow White
- Sunbright Yellow
- Victorian Blue

Other Supplies
- Inexpensive rug hook tool
- Sandpaper medium grit
- Tack cloth
- Loew Cornell #4 filbert brush
- Loew Cornell #4 flat brush
- Loew Cornell #18/0 liner brush
- Sealer or craft varnish

Painting the Hydrangeas

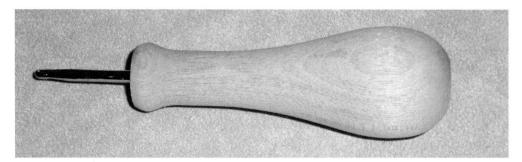

Sand the hook handle to give the paint a surface to which to adhere. Use the tack cloth to wipe all dust off. Then basecoat the handle with two thin coats of Victorian Blue, letting dry in between coats.

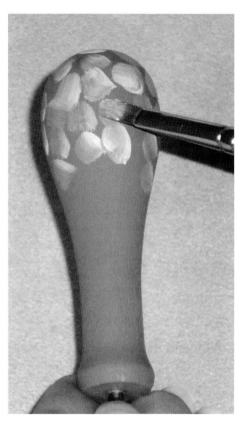

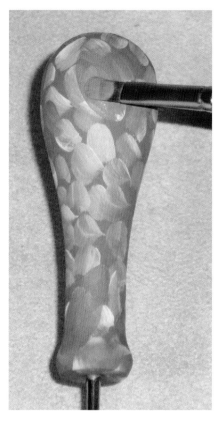

Pour out a small puddle of Sapphire Blue. Add a small bit of Snow White 4:1. Pick up a small dab of paint with the filbert and place; then drag slightly and lift off to make the small background petals.

With the Hauser Medium Green, draw on a few simple leaf shapes and basecoat. Shade with Hauser Dark Green and highlight with Hauser Light Green. *See Penny Rug Frame for directions on shading.* Highlighting is done the same as shading, but on the opposite side of the leaf. With a liner brush and watered down Hauser Light Green, make a vein through the center of the leaves.

With Sapphire and Snow White, paint four petals by drawing the brush towards the center. Dab the brush in the Sapphire or the Snow White to add a little shading to the petals; add individual petals in areas that look sparse. Hydrangeas don't have yellow dots in the middle, but I added them. It adds a little spark to the petals.

Give the handle several coats of sealer (varnish) following the directions on the bottle. Wait a couple of days to let the paint and sealer cure.

For the Pink Hydrangeas:

Basecoat the handle with Maroon, make the first layer of petals with Wild Rose, to make the petal quartets use Hydrangea Pink and Snow White, dabbing into the Wild Rose. Centers are Sunbright Yellow.

For the White Hydrangeas:

Basecoat with Eucalyptus, make the first layer of petals with Moss Green, to make the petal quartets use Antique White and White dabbing into the Moss Green. Centers are Sunbright Yellow.

Christmas Ornaments

Materials

Wool

- 1/8-yard White
- 1/8-yard Red
- 12" x 12" Green
- 10" x 10" Gold
- 6" x 6" Cream Wool

DMC Floss

- Blanc
- 321 Red
- 890 Pistachio Green, Ultra Dark
- 3822 Straw, Light
- 5282 Light Effects Metallic Gold

Other Supplies

- 20" x 20" Backing Fabric
- Fabric for back of ornaments
- Old CDs
- 15" of trim for each ornament
- Beads, charms, or other adornments
- Tacky glue
- Fiberfill
- Clothespins

Poinsettia

Peppermint Candy

Transfer patterns onto your backing fabric. *(Refer to "Transferring Your Pattern" in Chapter Two.)* I used a CD as my circle guide. Finish the edges, referring to "Finishing the Edges" in Chapter Two.

Following the pictures for color placement, hook pattern. On the Poinsettia pattern, the front leaves are labeled "A" and are hooked in white wool; the back leaves are labeled "B" and are hooked in cream.

Zigzag 1-2" around each ornament and cut away the excess.

Star

Turn edge under after zigzagging.

Sew the edge to the backing.

Spread tacky glue around the outside edge.

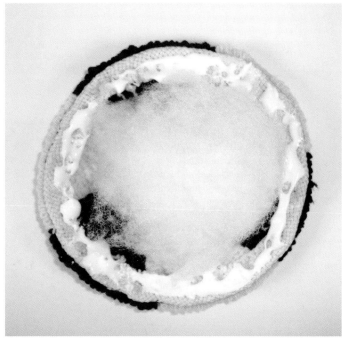

Add fiberfill in the center and place CD on top.

Clamp with clothespins and let dry.

Glue down tabs and back.

To Finish:

Remove the clothespins. Cut the back by tracing the CD on a piece of fabric or wool. Cut two pieces of trim approximately 3". Glue one at the top and one at the bottom of the CD. Spread glue over the rest of the CD and lay the back on top. Press gently with your fingers. Let dry.

Starting at the bottom, sew the trim around the circle with a whipstitch catching the front and back of the ornament.

Making the Tassle

You will need a piece of cardboard approximately 4" x 6" (a paperback book works well also). Choose the color flosses you want to use. I used floss that matched the trim I found.

• For the Poinsettia: I used 321 Red, 890 Pistachio Green Ultra Dark, and 3822 Straw Light.

• For the Peppermint Candy: I used Blanc 321 Red, Blanc, and 5282 Light Effects Metallic Gold.

• For the Star: I used 321 Red, 890 Pistachio Green Ultra Dark, and 5282 Light Effects Metallic Gold.

Gather the three floss colors (or however many you choose) and wrap them at the same time — between 12-18 times — around the cardboard. Place a rubber band near the top. Run a needle and thread through all the threads at the top and make a knot, catching all the floss.

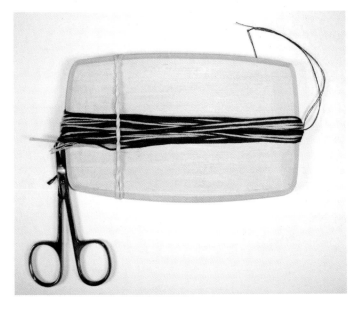

Bring the rubber band to the bottom and cut through the floss.

Gently pull the thread at the top and tie a thread approximately 1" down. Trim the end so all floss is even.

To finish, thread various beads and trinkets on the needle and tie to the loop at the bottom of the ornament.

Notes:

Appendix

Patterns

Christmas Ornaments:
Full size

Tongue

Penny

Fruit Rug Hooking:
Enlarge 122%

Welcome Thyme: Enlarge 284%

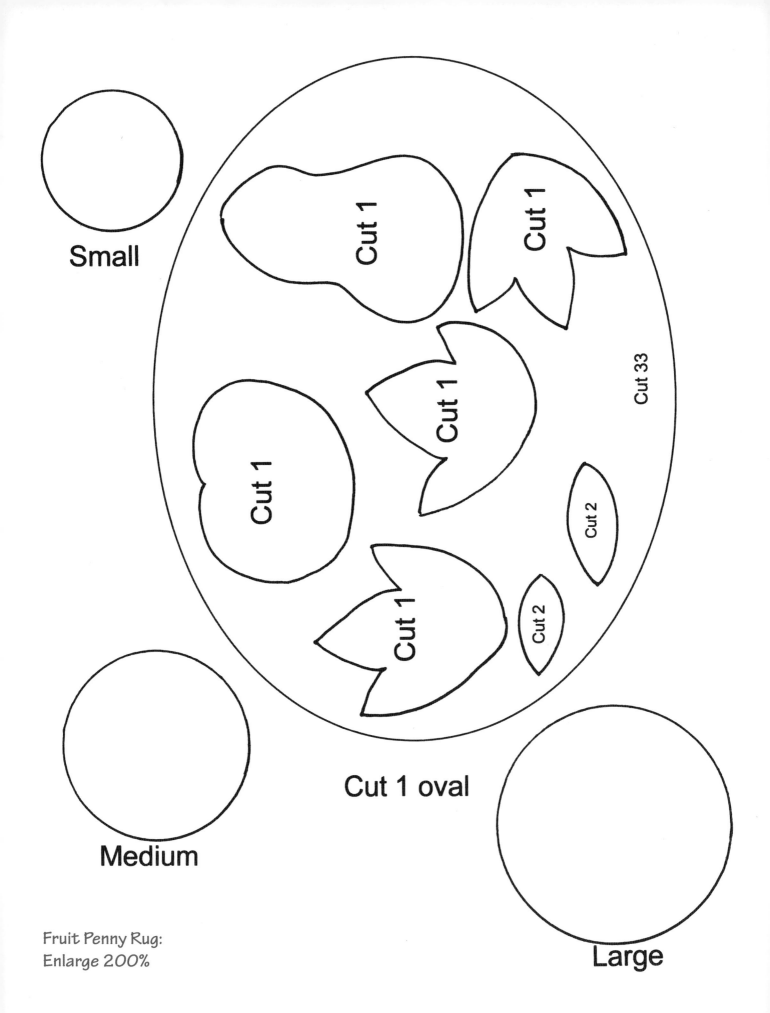

Small

Cut 1

Cut 1

Cut 1

Cut 33

Cut 1

Cut 2

Cut 1

Cut 2

Medium

Cut 1 oval

Large

Fruit Penny Rug:
Enlarge 200%

102

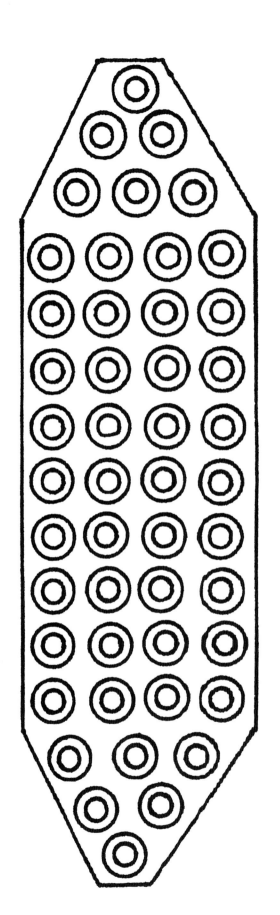

Pennies from Heaven Rug:
Enlarge 500%

Left:
Crows on Watermelon Hooked Rug:
Enlarge 344%

Crows on Watermelon Wool Applique:
Enlarge 200%

Lighthouse Rug Hooking/Penny Rug:
Enlarge 133%

Right:
Loden:
Enlarge 500%

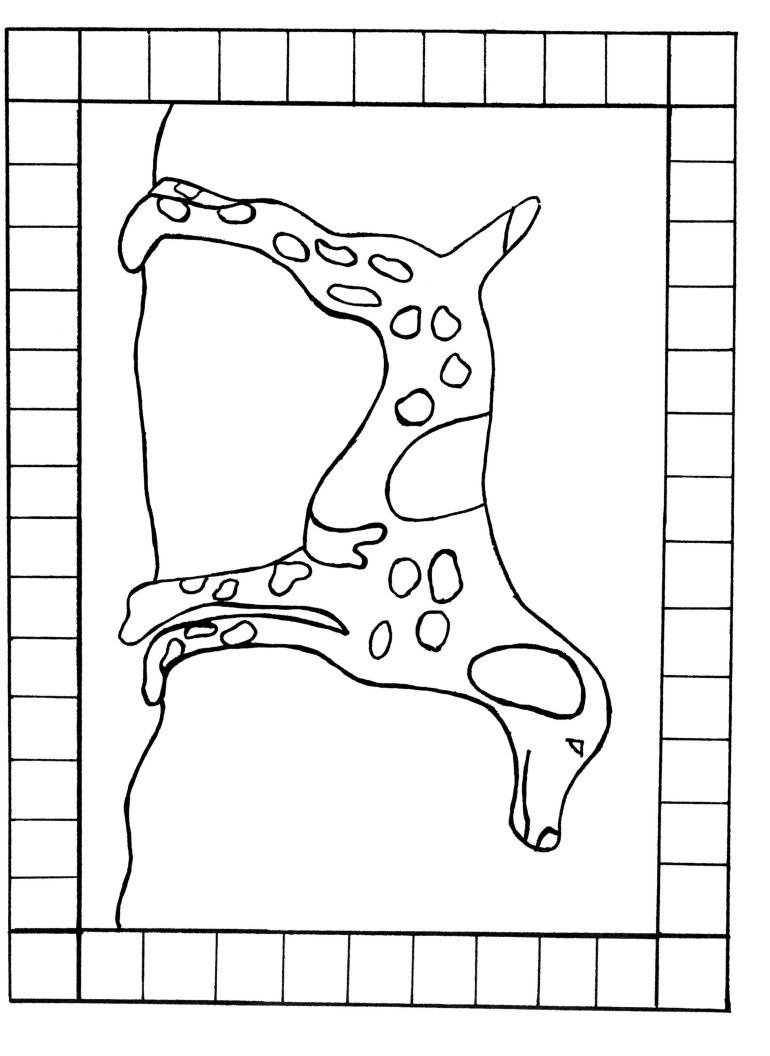

Enlarge 200%

FULL SIZE

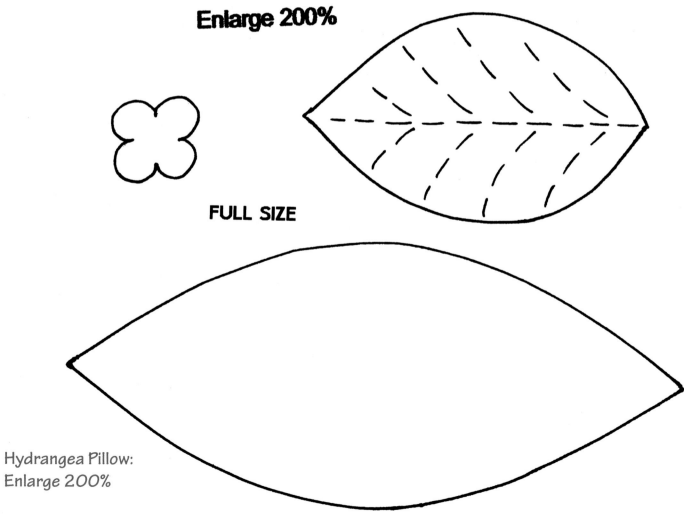

Hydrangea Pillow:
Enlarge 200%

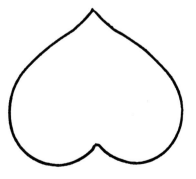

Pineapple Rug Hooking/Wool Appliqué:
Enlarge 233%

References

Magazines

ATHA/Association of Traditional Hooking Artists
Joan Cahill, Membership Chairman
600 Maple Street
Endicott, NY 13760
607-748-7588
www.atharugs.com

Rug Hooking Magazine
1300 Market Street, Suite 202
Leymoyne, PA 17043-1420
800-233-9055
www.rughookingonline.com

The Wool Street Journal
312 North Custer
Colorado Springs, CO 80903
888-784-5667
woolstreetjournal.com

Books

~ *The Art of Rug Hooking* (Anne D. Mather)
~ *Purely Primitive: Hooked Rugs from Wool, Yarn, and Homespun Scraps* (Pat Cross)
~ *Secrets of Finishing Hooked Rugs* (Margaret Siano with Susan Huxley)
~ *Wooley Fox American Folk Art Rug Hooking*

Resources

Ault's Rug Hooking Store
4515 Laser Road
Shelby, Ohio 44875
419-347-9957
866-659-1752
www.aults.com
Cutters, hooks, wool, and more

Dorr Mill Store
PO Box 88
Guild, NH 03754
800-846-3677
www.dorrmillstore.com
Dyeing supplies, hooks, and wool

Halcyon Yarn
12 School Street
Bath, ME 04530
800-341-0282
www.halcyonyarn.com
*Yarn, hooks, backing fabrics, and
dyeing supplies*

Harry M. Fraser Company
433 Duggins Road
Stoneville, NC 27049
336-673-9830
www.fraserrugs.com
Cutters, hooks, and backing fabrics

Pro Chemical & Dye
PO Box 14
Somerset, MA 02726
800-2-BUY-DYE
www.prochemical.com
Dyeing supplies

W. Cushing & Company
P.O. Box 351
21 North Street
Kennebunkport, ME 04046
www.wcushing.com
*Dyeing supplies, hooks, backing fabrics,
and more*

Heavenly Heart Creations
Kim Hogue, CDA
150 South Main Street
Bellingham, MA 02019
508-883-9183
kihogue@comcast.net
Penny Rug Frame

Notes: